A Piece of My Puzzle

Through the Eyes and Heart of a Single Mother Raising a Child with Autism

---

By Precious Tameka Weatherspoon

A Piece of My Puzzle: Through the Eyes and Heart of a Single Mother Raising a Child with Autism

Copyright © 2018 by Precious Weatherspoon

For inquiries please contact:

ISpeak Publishing Services

http://www.tiffanysgreene.com

http://www.ispeakpublishing.com

Contact the Publisher via email: tiffanysgreene@gmail.com

Contact the Author via email: piecestomypuzzle2014@gmail.com

All rights reserved. No part of this book may be reproduced, stored in a retrieved system, or transmitted in any form or by any means, electronic, mechanical, photocopying, recording, scanning, or otherwise, without the prior written permission of the author.

All Scriptures come from the New International Standard, International Version and the English Standard Version (ESV) King James Version (KJV) New International Version (NIV) unless otherwise indicated.

Disclaimer

All the material contained in this book is provided for educational and informational purposes only. No responsibility can be taken for any results or outcomes resulting from the use of this material.

While every attempt has been made to provide information that is both accurate and effective, the author does not assume any responsibility for the accuracy or use/misuse of this information.

Printed in the United States of America

ISBN 13: 978-0-692-11683-8

ISBN 10: 0692116834

ISpeak Publishing Service

www.tiffanysgreene.com

www.ispeakpublishing.com

Little Rock, AR.

501-519-6996

Table of Contents

Introduction 1
Prologue 2
Finally — My Son 3
The Diagnosis and Shutting Down 7
The Hurt and the Hate 12
Going Numb 16
Envying Other Moms with Sons 21
The Words "Normal" and "Special" 26
It's OK to *Not* be OK All the Time 29
Living Life as an Example 35
Balancing Life with Your Other Kids 39
Dating as a Single Mom with a Special-Needs Child 42
Get Off the Guilt Train 46
Taking It One Day at a Time 50
Being Open to New Ways of Thinking and Reacting 54
Listening Without Words 57
Autism Is a Journey! Wear Your Seat Belt 60
Putting the Pieces Together 63
Finding Peace and Living Life 65
Bibliography 68

ACKNOWLEDGMENTS

First and foremost, I give all praises and thanks to God for guiding me throughout this entire writing process. I am one of His most stubborn children, but He has never given up on me. For that alone, I am forever thankful for His mercy and grace.

I want to thank my three children — from the eldest to the youngest, Darryana, Jayla and Caleb — for allowing Mommy to have writing time each day while they entertained and helped each other. Thank you, babies, for being everything Mommy needed to keep moving forward and for teaching me what it looks like, feels like, and means to love unconditionally.

I want to thank, from the bottom of my heart, my own sweet mommy, who always prayed for me and our Caleb. I call her my behind-the-scenes operator. I felt many times my prayers were not making it to God, but my mommy had something extra-special about hers. When I talked to her and she prayed with and for me, I knew I was going to be OK.

My sister Tanisha and I should have been twins. We have a bond that most people will never understand. Sometimes it throws me for a loop, but that's OK. Tanisha, thank you for being not just my sister, but my best friend and protector. I love you, girl, and I appreciate everything you do.

In life, you sometimes meet very special people with whom you can truly bond and connect. It's rare, but it happens, and it happened for me with my friend and spiritual sister, Tammie. I thank God every day for this beautiful soul. I wanted to give up so many times when I felt I was at my lowest, but Tammie extended words of encouragement and truth and helped me to stand again. Tammie, you are truly the definition of a spiritual sister.

We all have that one friend who is always ready to get physical, if need be, with anyone who threatens us. Janea Monique has been such a friend. I have known this beautiful woman for years and she has always had my back *and* front, no matter what! She is ready even when I don't need her to be. I love you, Janea, and I am thankful that you are my "soldier girl" ... and much more.

It is a blessing to have a best friend from your childhood school days who is still in your life. For me that friend is Likera, also known as Kera G. Thank you, Kera, for being my friend. When we are old and gray, we will be nursing-home roommates, giving everyone a tough time together as we share life stories and try to figure out why this or that happened (LOL). I love you, Kera. Thank you for being my best friend, always.

The next person I want to thank is my big brother Corey (Shea). During what seemed like the toughest times in my life, my brother could not physically be present to help ... but, via letters and visits, he was the best at letting his little sister vent, cry, and ask him thousands of questions I'm sure were silly to him. Thank you, Shea, for encouraging and uplifting me when I needed it the most, all while you were far away from family and home. I appreciate every conversation with you, bro! You just don't know how much it meant for you to take the time to listen to me. I love you.

I also want to thank my boyfriend and best friend, James, for being everything I needed during my time of healing, learning patience, learning to live in the present moment, and learning to love again. You are, and will always be, my superman and the yin to my yang.

I am forever grateful for this next individual, Pastor Tiffany Greene-Moorer, who is not only my spiritual leader but my book publisher (Ispeak Publishing). I do not always see what she sees in me, but one thing is for sure: I appreciate the genuine care, patience and love she gives me. I am thankful to have Pastor Tiffany in many of roles in my life. Best of all, she is simply herself and allows me to be me unapologetically. I also want to express my sincerest appreciation to my editor, Helaine R. Williams of Make It Plain Ministries.

There are so many more people I want to thank, but I do not want to leave anyone out. So, from the bottom of my heart I sincerely thank each one of you who prayed, encouraged and supported my Caleb and me through our journey with autism, serving as a great piece to our team. We love you guys so much! No deed you did was ever small!

Sincerely, Precious

Introduction

I still remember how I felt when, after struggling financially for seven years, I was able to make enough extra money to visit my therapist ... ironically, the very same therapist my ex-boyfriend and I had seen for couples counseling. I knew I could not afford to see her on a much-needed regular basis. But she was a familiar face and she knew some of my past, so I was happy that she responded to my request to visit her for a different matter after so many years had passed by.

I remember attempting to unload all my pain on her in one hour's session. It was like I was trying to get out of my head all the feelings that were holding me hostage, and put them into words. She was so patient with me. She simply walked over and asked if she could give me a hug. "I know you are tired; I see it," she said. In that moment, I knew my pain was no longer simply bottled up inside me; it now had made its presence on the outside.

My therapist asked only one thing from me. She requested that I start writing. "It doesn't have to make sense; just write," she said. And I did. Writing was the beginning of my release. It was my catharsis. No longer was I holding everything in.

Now hear me clearly, please. This is not a book with which I'm trying to convince you to feel sorry for me or my son, Caleb. This isn't even a book where good guys and bad guys are defined. This is my story ... my life, through my eyes and heart, as a single parent on a journey of autism with my family.

Precious Tameka Weatherspoon

Prologue

Be strong and courageous. Do not be afraid or terrified because of them, for the LORD your God goes with you; he will never leave you nor forsake you.

— Deuteronomy 31:6 (NIV)

A note from a mother's heart …

I gave birth to you, but you came with no instructions. All I knew was that I loved you long before I saw you. I know I made some mistakes, and for that I am so sorry. I was doing the best I could with what I knew. Everything I did for you I did from love. You are my son, my life, my dreams for tomorrow. I will always love and protect you, Caleb Lamar Harris.

Finally — My Son

"It's definitely a boy!" the doctor assured me.

My smile couldn't have been any bigger. I was happy at the thought of sharing with my daughters, Darryana and Jayla, the news that they would be big sisters very soon.

Shortly after ending a five-year relationship with a previous boyfriend, I began seeing my son's dad and soon became pregnant. I had heartburn from hell and gained a lot of weight, but I had no complications except for a scary situation that occurred one night at the home of my sister Tanisha. (Tanisha's house had pretty much turned into my house. I hated staying home for many reasons, one being that I had stairs in my house, and stairs plus a very pregnant woman are not a great combination.)

This night, I kept feeling a weird pressure in my lower stomach, followed by some of the worst cramps I'd ever experienced. I went to the restroom and noticed I was bleeding heavily. Next thing I knew I was headed to the hospital, where they checked me out. The baby was OK at that moment, I was told, but I could possibly be having a miscarriage. I was advised to take it easy, which meant bed rest.

I cried so much at the thought of losing another baby. I have babies who are now in heaven, so I needed this baby to make it! Every little movement made me love him even more. His little kicks hurt, but I appreciated them; they let me know my baby was alive.

At the time, I just *knew* I was in love with my son's dad. There was no one else for me. This guy had my heart, and I was carrying his son. I had already told myself, "Girl, you are on Baby Daddy Number 3, so do whatever you need to do to keep him, even if he is only halfway in you guys' lives!" Thoughts of people talking bothered me so much. I could literally hear them saying, "She must be crazy. She can't keep a man, but she sure can make babies!" I'm sure more than that was said. For the record, no girl ever *plans* to be a single parent, especially not for the third time. I'd literally lost myself while trying to hold onto someone who clearly did not love or respect me at all. I was in trouble, and my baby boy had not even made it into this world yet.

At 5:15 a.m. March 21, 2014 — after 14 long hours of labor — I gave birth to an 8-pound, 4-ounce baby boy I named Caleb Lamar Harris. At that moment, everything was perfect. I did not care who was there or who wasn't. All I could see was this perfect little boy, and he belonged to me! I fell in love even deeper.

Caleb's dad and I continued our roller-coaster relationship. I just could not understand why we could not get it together. He would help with Caleb when we were on good terms. Caleb was a mommy's boy — and I'll admit he was spoiled, as the older people would say — but his dad was good with him. I loved seeing them bond. But as soon as his dad and I were on bad terms, it was like we didn't exist to him. You would think this alone would have given me the strength to let this man go, but it didn't. You can say it … I was beyond weak and pathetic. I would go through days, sometimes months, literally anticipating the moment he would pop up or call as if he hadn't been gone all that time.

A Piece of My Puzzle

I was far from perfect, but I never cheated on this man; I wouldn't dare entertain anyone else. The crazy part about it was, we never formally announced that we were together; we just went through the motions.

Caleb, meanwhile, was growing up fast. I made sure to capture every moment possible. Looking back, I'm glad I did. I took pictures and shot videos galore; my son always had a camera in his face. Caleb, to me, was the smartest baby ever. He knew all his ABC's and could spell his name in song. He could even count to 10 before his first birthday. And he loved music. I lived for the eye contact he'd make, followed by that sweet, angelic smile.

As Caleb's first birthday drew near, he began getting sick all the time. His little body could not recover from one illness before another came on him. He suffered from severe allergies and reoccurring ear infections, and constantly needed breathing treatments. We tried every antibiotic and steroid — you name, it we tried it — but nothing seemed to be working. Caleb was a fighter, but when he was sick, it broke my heart.

My sweet baby boy had his first birthday. Fortunately, his party was everything I'd planned and more. Both sides of his family were in attendance. No matter what was going on with me, family would always be important, so to see everyone there made me happy.

Soon afterward, Caleb received his first-year vaccinations and his first set of ear tubes. I had no fears except the natural fear of my baby being put to sleep for surgery. Little did I know, that was going to be the least of my worries.

Caleb continued to deal with his illnesses. One doctor told me that Caleb was just a sickly child and that he would outgrow these illnesses one day. Seriously? I felt that he was inconsiderate, unprofessional, and a failure at reassuring a mother who was doing everything on her end to make sure her baby boy was well. So, I made the decision to move myself and my children from Jonesboro, Ark. to little Rock, Ark. I had lived there as a child with my sister Tanisha, my parents and with my daughters when they were younger. I knew Little Rock had some great doctors; I needed answers for my baby. And I needed a change of scenery. The move was my "out of sight, out of mind" getaway from the stress of Caleb's dad's finale exit. Jonesboro was not a place I wanted to be anymore, so I was more than ready to leave.

The Diagnosis and Shutting Down

So, there I was, a single parent of three, recently moved, trying to work a full-time job *and* go to school ... while dealing with a sick toddler. To say that all this was stressful would be an understatement.

I know what you're probably thinking at this point: "Precious, enough of this complaining! I know plenty of women who have been in your shoes and gotten the job done." That may be true, but as I had not properly unloaded my previous burdens before the new ones had presented themselves, I felt especially weighed down as I tried to balance it all. Caleb's health was showing no signs of improvement. I felt guilty because most of my time was given to Caleb, and I did not want my daughters to feel that they weren't important.

Shortly after Caleb's first-year vaccinations, I began to notice that he made little to no eye contact. Something just seemed off with my baby boy, and I couldn't pinpoint it. Was it the vaccinations? That's a debate within itself ... an exhausting debate, to say the least. At this time, we'd switched doctors because Caleb's health checkups had become a frustrating repeat of those in Jonesboro.

I began working at Pediatrics Plus, a school for special-needs children in Little Rock. I have always worked with special-needs children and have been in the childcare field in general for more than 16 years. But something was different about this place. A good feeling came over me the first day I entered the building.

My Caleb was getting ready to turn 2 soon, and I was trying to get him enrolled so I could have him there with me. It got even better: One day, as I was talking with the school nurse about finding Caleb another doctor, she suggested I check into All For Kids Pediatrics Clinic, also in Little Rock. She helped me make a smooth transition there. And Dr. Dawn Martin of All For Kids was nothing short of heaven sent. She went straight to work getting me answers for my baby boy. There was a lot to take in, and the appointments seemed never-ending, but it felt good to see that someone genuinely cared for my child. After a few checkups, Dr. Martin suggested I take Caleb to the city's James Dennis Developmental Center for development testing. I did so.

On May 31, 2015, my only son, for whom I had prayed for so many times, was diagnosed with autism. My heart broke into a million pieces. I'd gone alone to that evaluation and diagnosis and I left feeling even more alone. I could not process what was happening.

Let me stop to explain that there are three distinct types of what are known as autism spectrum disorders: **Asperger's syndrome**; **pervasive developmental disorder**, or **PDD-NOS**; and **autistic disorder.**

Asperger's syndrome is at the milder end of the autism spectrum. A person with Asperger's can handle his daily life independently. He may be very focused on a certain topic of interest, and discuss it nonstop. He has a much harder time socially.

PDD-NOS — a mouthful of a diagnosis — includes most individuals whose autism is more severe than Asperger's syndrome, but not as severe as autistic disorder.

A Piece of My Puzzle

Autistic disorder (also called "classic" autism) is what most people think of when hearing the word "autism." People with autistic disorder usually have significant language delays, social and communication challenges, and unusual behaviors and interests. This is what my Caleb was diagnosed with.

Autism spectrum disorders include social, communication, and behavioral challenges. These problems can be mild, severe, or somewhere in between. Early diagnosis is extremely important, because early treatment can make an enormous impact and difference for the individual.

(This may be a lot to grasp, but simply doing your research and asking questions will help you to better understand.)

Devastated at Caleb's diagnosis, I cried myself to sleep that night. The next day, I went to work with swollen eyes and cried even more. I could not get myself together. I'll be honest: It put a strain on my relationship with my family. Everyone knows that my mommy, my sister and I have always been close and have always stuck by each other's side; we lived no more than 15 minutes from each other. But life seemed to be pulling us all in different directions at that time. I had never felt more alone in my life. I knew that they loved Caleb and me, but it was as if they just didn't get it. And the "it," in my mind, was everything.

The good thing is that I met some amazing supervisors, coworkers and therapists while working at Pediatrics Plus. They were an immense help to me as I began this autism journey with my Caleb; I was blessed with a lot of useful resources. So I told myself I was OK and that I could handle Caleb's condition.

But then I started beating myself up, wondering what I had done wrong for this to happen. I became so depressed that all I did was work, go home, go through the motions of taking care of my kids, and cry ... every single day, without fail. I was far from OK. I felt that no one really understood my situation and that venting too much about it would make me a crybaby. I'd had my fair-share days of being weak, so I decided to try to keep it all in. That only resulted in me lashing out at people I cared about ... not only family members, but potential friends and relationship partners. I could not see a light at the end of my tunnel; it was darkened with anger, frustration, hopelessness, regret, what-ifs, should-haves and but-whys.

I have dealt with different issues in the past and overcome them — or, I might say, survived them — but this was different. It was not just me being affected; my sweet baby boy and my daughters were also affected. Our world would never be the same. We would have to adapt and make sacrifices.

Everywhere I turned, I heard or saw that word ... AUTISM. Each time, it felt like needles being drilled into my eyes and ears. I hated to say the word. I didn't want others to say it. I told myself that Caleb was still young and was just growing and developing at his own pace; he still could, as society would say, BE NORMAL.

Embarrassed and angry that I was going through this alone, I attempted to reach out to Caleb's dad on several occasions. I got no response. I then did the unthinkable: I turned away from God. I honestly felt I had done something horrible and that my poor, sweet, innocent baby boy was paying for it. So, I figured, why should I bother to have faith and pray to God? He'd seen every night I'd been awake with Caleb when he was sick, suffering from sensory overload or unable to sleep. He'd heard every cry.

A Piece of My Puzzle

I had prayed so much and so hard. I felt that God had watched me go through this horrible ordeal with my son and done nothing about it. In my mind, He did not care about me.

So, whenever I heard a church song on the radio, I turned it off. When someone invited me to church I declined, using the excuse that the noise hurt Caleb's ears and he couldn't sit for extended periods of time.

Reflection

She loved hard. She remained quiet on the outside. She forgave, multiple times. She prayed. She cried ... oh, how she cried! She over-thought thoughts, battled battles, and fought wars no one knew about. She was happy one minute, sad the next as she remembered the pain, the loss, the hurt, the anger, the frustration, the emptiness, the what-ifs.

Then she grew tired and decided "no more" ... no more feelings, no more love, no more giving chances. She turned it all off for good, allowing her heart to turn black and cold. That woman who once was, was no longer. And she was never coming back.

To Be Continued ...

Come to me, all who labor and are heavy laden, and I will give you rest. Take my yoke upon you, and learn from me, for I am gentle and lowly in heart, and you will find rest for your souls. For my yoke is easy, and my burden is light.

— Matthew 11:28-30 (ESV)

The Hurt and the Hate

Because revenge is a very known feeling in American culture, there's a certain element of an eye for an eye. There's the saying, 'Be careful what you wish for, you might get it.' When you wish for revenge, and you think you've gotten it, what happens then? Revenge is just a really good drive for drama and good action.

— *Niels Arden Oplev*

I was totally wrapped up in my hurt over Caleb's diagnosis, and that hurt began to take a toll on everyone else. My family walked on eggshells around me. I hated seeing that, but at the same time, I did not want them or anyone else to bother me. I felt I was merely existing, not living. I was truly in an unhealthy place. Even sleep brought no peace; my dreams reflected my reality. I wanted someone, *anyone*, to feel the hurt I was feeling … and I didn't care who that was.

My stress and exhaustion began to take its toll on my body. I would hear people make remarks about being "depressed" because their favorite TV show didn't come on, or their favorite restaurant no longer offered their favorite lunch special. I, on the other hand, truly *was* suffering. I hated feeling as though I were on a seesaw and could not get off. My emotions were up or down; there was no in-between. I just needed a minute to *not* feel as though I were backed in a corner.

A Piece of My Puzzle

My dear mommy would constantly pray over me and tell me, "It will get better, Baby Girl. Just hang in there." *She wasn't going through what I was going through,* I'd think. *How did she know I was going to be OK?* Mommy spoke of her unmovable faith. Well, I had given that up already, so I needed her to come up with something else. I gave all my energy to my anger and hurt; I didn't even *try* to be positive. I hated these feelings but did nothing to change them. If I can be honest, I *wanted* to be angry and hurt. I *wanted* to hate people and this entire situation.

Ironically, watching my baby boy every day, I saw that he had a peace about him. Now don't get me wrong; his behavior could be challenging, and his meltdowns could be epic. But when he was just playing or otherwise busying himself, he looked like the happiest child in the world. He wasn't worried about anything except what he was doing right then and there. *Why couldn't I be more like Caleb?* I wondered. *If I choose to stay quiet about everything going on, I feel like I'm being weak. But if I speak up, I'll come off as crazy and full of drama.* So, saying what was on my mind was not an option.

I am, to be honest, an overthinker. And I concluded that the thing I needed to do in this situation was silently scream out, and cry alone when no one is around. Eventually, I came to the realization that I needed God. Exhaling, I looked up and asked the Lord to help me.

My daughters had been so patient and helpful. I felt bad because they had taken on so many responsibilities and sacrificed so much. I found myself consistently apologizing to them. I did not want them to feel as though they had to stop being kids. I would try to take time to have mommy-daughter conversations with them, explaining how important it was to work hard for everything they wanted in life; to always show kindness; to take their time getting to know people; to base any future relationships on the other person's character and potential, rather than their looks or what they had to offer materially; and to always pray for discernment.

I would always end our talks with my daughters by saying, "Guess what?"

"We know, Mommy — you love us!" they'd reply.

It was our thing, and I felt I could not possibly say those words to them enough. I wanted to make sure I was giving them my all.

Again, things were not easy for my daughters. My youngest daughter began acting out in school ... nothing major, but enough to get my attention. I honestly think that was her way of saying "Hello, you have two other kids who also need you." But. overall, they adapted to change well. Not one time did they feel sorry for Caleb or treat him like he had a disability. To them he was just their little brother, and they loved him unconditionally.

A year after Caleb's diagnosis, I feared I was on the verge of losing my job because he was sick so much and had so many appointments, evaluations, sleep studies and surgeries. But as I said before, I'd felt a welcoming peace when I first entered the building of Pediatrics Plus ... and that feeling turned out to be justified. I thank God for the compassion and patience my supervisors showed me. I appreciate everything they did for me while I was employed there, especially considering how completely in over my head I was.

I have always agreed with those who say it's never fair to legally seek child support from a man for the wrong reasons. I'll be honest: I was angry and hurt when I decided to go after Caleb's dad for child support, but I also had good reason to do so. Time was passing. It had been the longest he'd gone without performing what I call his "groundhog trick" — popping up randomly to check on his son. He had two other children by two other women and was on the hook to pay child support for them also. I did not ask him for anything extra financially, and it was no longer about my feelings for him or about us. I just wanted him to be physically present and consistent in helping with Caleb, because I *needed* help. I needed a break just to think and process things clearly ... at the time I made the decision to seek action against his dad, Caleb had just had surgery on his tonsils, adenoids, and ear tubes replaced all in one day.

Also, I didn't want to give Caleb's dad a reason to say I did not do my part to keep him updated or involved in Caleb's life. I presented opportunities for him to be in his son's life; matter of fact, I *allowed* him to treat his relationship with my baby like a revolving door. *Maybe he just doesn't know how to come back around ... or what he should be saying or doing*, I went so far as to think. So each time we spoke I never once said, "You've been gone," "You've missed so much," or "You are so wrong." I simply gave him updates about Caleb and created opportunities for him to spend time with him. Once again, I was being the bigger person and making excuses for him and his behavior. I tried to tell myself over and over that it didn't matter and hoped that soon I would come to really believe that.

For God, who said, "Let light shine out of darkness," made his light shine in our hearts to give us the light of the knowledge of God's glory displayed in the face of Christ.

— 2 Corinthians 4:6, NIV

Going Numb

I've felt happiness at its greatest; and I've felt depressed to the core; but there's nothing worse than being numb and feeling no more.

— Unknown

I went from wearing my anger and hurt on my sleeve to trying to convince myself and others that I was in control and couldn't care less about all the messed-up things going on in my life. I did not want anyone looking at me with pity because I was this 33-year-old single woman with three kids ... no thank you. How does that saying go? "Fake it until you make it." Yes, I tried to do that and yes, it was another of my epic fails. I was smiling, repeating uplifting quotes and taking lots of pretty pictures of my family and me. But all the while, behind closed doors, I was a hot mess.

I found myself one day sitting in my car, trying to catch a few moments for myself and make sense of where I was in my life ... you know, one of those "recap" moments where you try to self-evaluate. I eventually decided I needed what is popularly known as an adult beverage, so I drove to the liquor store and found the perfect numbing drink. Those trips continued. One wine in particular did a great job of making me feel calm, but when I needed something stronger I had to have my vodka. Self-medicating with alcohol felt so good ... that is, until the bottles were empty. It proved to be only a temporary numbness. I needed something stronger to keep me from crying myself to sleep, concluding that everything I was going through was completely my fault.

I also needed something to keep me from thinking I wasn't good enough to have, or keep, a man. My weight had always gone up and down, but after my son I'd noticed that the weight wasn't leaving as fast. So I was now considered a "curvy" girl. However, I was still attractive enough that I could post a picture and get a lot of attention from men. I would be lying if I said it didn't make me feel good to receive attention, even if that attention sometimes came from males who had no business giving it. My confidence hadn't been at its best in a while, so alcohol and male attention were my ways of trying to stay numb. They were a very bad combination, I might add, but it was a high from which I didn't want to come down. When the alcohol took over and the men were looking, I wasn't thinking about being good enough, or raising three kids by myself. I wasn't thinking anything except, *Girl, you look damn good to them!* These men were lusting after me, and alcohol was like the icing on the cake.

Of course I had it all wrong and was moving backward instead of forward. These guys only saw my picture. They had no idea I was a complete mess inside and getting worse by the moment. I had forgotten that I'd been raised to have respect for myself ... and that not only did I represent *me*, I was also a reflection of my loved ones and everyone who cared about me.

I will not lie and say I woke up and had an epiphany. I knew I was going about this situation in the wrong way. I had made this more about me than about Caleb and his diagnosis. I needed to get it together. I still wasn't in church like I should have been. I'd stopped being mad at God; I was praying and listening to gospel music again; but I still had not gotten on the right path. I honestly loved the feeling of *not* feeling. It felt good to have options when it came to men who wanted my attention, and the alcohol was like a boost of liquid courage. I was living life as though I were a reckless teenager again. The thing I had to come to understand was that all this self-medicating was only a temporary fix.

I finally got to a point where I was tired of numbing myself. When it came to living, I wanted the real thing, I decided. I took a break from social media and substituted my adult beverages for writing and working out. Let me tell you, it was not easy ... especially for someone who, up to this point in her life, had felt like she needed male attention and alcohol. And that was not the worst. It broke my heart when I realized that I was attempting to escape my reality ... a reality in which I was blessed with three beautiful children who deserved me at my best. I was their primary role model and here I was, messing it all up My reality was that I was able to work and provide for my kids. All their needs were being met, as well as most of their wants. But I could not see any of that, because I was wrapped up in my own mess. I had cried a lot, but I had never *really* cried ... and screamed ... and released everything I was feeling. I was still holding on to my pain. I was still in an unhealthy place, and it wasn't going to change if I kept on this way.

"God never allows pain without a purpose in the lives of His children," according to the late Jerry Bridges, evangelical Christian author, whose quotes appear at the website Christian Quotes (www.Christianquotes.info). "He never allows Satan, nor circumstances, nor any ill-intending person to afflict us unless He uses that affliction for our good. God never wastes pain. He always causes it to work together for our ultimate good, the good

A Piece of My Puzzle

of conforming us more to the likeness of His Son." Bridges based this passage on Romans 8:28-29: *And we know that for those who love God all things work together for good, for those who are called according to his purpose. For those whom he foreknew he also predestined to be conformed to the image of his Son, in order that he might be the firstborn among many brothers* (ESV).

This passage is what we call right on time, and very relatable for me. I had to acknowledge everything that was going on with me in order to properly deal with it all. I learned there are two types of forgiveness. There's the type in which you offer the forgiven one another chance. Then there is the other kind, the one I needed so much to perfect: the type in which you forgive and move on without that person.

Bottom line was, I still was carrying around all those unanswered questions about Caleb's father — why did he leave me to raise our son alone? How is he able to wake up each day, go about his life, and not reach out to check on his son? I really loved this man and thought, at one point, that he felt the same about me. And it wasn't just about us; we had a child who was now 3 years old! I hated the fact that even after all this time had passed, I still had these come-and-go feelings for him. I could not understand why I could not just get over him already. I exhausted every avenue trying to do so. I had given so much of *me* to him, and in return he'd given me anger, frustration, hurt and trust issues! I had many people reassure me that I was doing a kick-butt job and that I shouldn't even be worried about him; he wasn't worth it. Why could I not stay consistent with my feelings? I needed help.

... Until you heal the wounds of your past, you are going to bleed. You can bandage the bleeding with food, with alcohol, with drugs, with work, with cigarettes, with sex, but eventually, it will all ooze through and stain your life. You must find the strength to open the wounds, stick your hands inside, pull out the core of the pain that is holding you in your past, the memories, and make peace with them.

— *Iyanla Vanzant*

Envying Other Moms with Sons

As parents, we not only want the absolute best for our children; we instinctively strive to create a successful life for them.

My desire for Caleb to have the best in life was a source of frustration ... and a source of envy. I would see moms taking their sons to football practice, basketball practice — any "boy" sport that required physical touch — and I would become angry and depressed. In my mind, my Caleb would never be interested in any of those things. When I found out I was expecting a son, the first thing I'd decided was that I was going to be that crazy mom in the bleachers, wearing a personalized shirt and cheering my kid on louder than everyone else. If he got hurt while playing, everybody would know I was upset! Now, I'd concluded that Caleb would never be interested in any of those sports. And that upset me.

Before Caleb went through autistic regression (a term used when a child appears to develop typically but then starts to lose speech and social skills, usually between the ages of 15 and 30 months), he, along with my daughters, would call me all the time — "Mama ... Mama ... Mama!" — until I told them, "Enough! Stop! You're not allowed to say it for at least five minutes!" Now, I found myself wishing I had simply enjoyed hearing Caleb's little voice saying "Mama." I hardly get to hear him say it now unless he is prompted, and he feels like it. All too often I hear parents telling their children, "I wish you would stop calling me/

saying my name," and it breaks my heart. I believe so many parents take for granted their children's ability to verbally communicate with them.

I was so focused in on what Caleb *couldn't* do and might not ever be able to do. I was looking so far into the future that it was literally making me crazy. I'd already chosen not to like the boys at school; I assumed they would be mean and cruel to my Caleb because he did not socialize with them the way they thought he should have. I could already see me having altercations with parents of these boys because of the parents' attitude that "they were just being boys." I could see the girls rejecting my Caleb because he seemed so different.

In fact, I was already considering avoiding the entire public-school thing and homeschooling Caleb … and, again, he was only 3!

I know you're thinking that this mommy needed to take a chill pill or two. But these are normal fears for any parent with a special-needs child. I'm not saying that a parent of an able-bodied child doesn't have concerns … but when you have a child with special needs, there's a level of concern that's hard to explain.

I was going about things all wrong, though. I was playing scary scenarios out in my mind and putting limits on Caleb. I was not a prophet, nor was I God; therefore, I could not predict Caleb's future. I simply was getting all worked up about things that weren't even close to happening. I wanted my son to be treated kindly and fairly, to say the least, and I knew that wasn't going to happen all the time. And although I vowed to protect Caleb, I knew I could not be around him every second of the day. That's when this mommy's faith needed to kick in fast. I needed to believe there were decent, caring, compassionate people in this world, and that they would cross paths with my Caleb at the right time. (If by chance Caleb runs across a bully or some other lost individual, my prayer is that his presence alone will melt that person's heart and inspire him to treat Caleb with kindness.)

To be honest, it took me a long time to acknowledge that I was envious of parents of little boys who had no special needs. I felt like that kid who had asked Santa Claus for a special Christmas gift ... then, when I finally received what I had waited for so long and wanted so very much, discovered that the gift had arrived with no instructions to make it work properly. That alone really hurt my feelings. To top it off, I had nobody (or so I thought) to *help me* to get the gift to work.

Of course, I had made so many plans for what I would do with this special gift ... but how does that saying go? "If you want to make God laugh, tell Him your plans." The point is that we should keep an attitude of humility. Boy, did I have to learn the hard way that I am not in control ... God is!

My envy was doing nothing for me or my family except robbing us of precious time — time I should have spent creating lifelong memories with my son. Again, I was so focused on what Caleb would *not* be able to do, I was missing out on things he *was* able to do ... and do very well at that. When I least expected it but needed it the most, my son would walk up to me, get in my face and give me a kiss. It's argued that autistic children do not show emotions appropriately or respond appropriately; I wholeheartedly disagree. Those tender moments Caleb shares with me, my family and others always brighten our days and make us feel better ... and they are always right on time.

At the age of 2, my Caleb could operate a computer tablet, laptop computer and smart TV better than this 32-year-old woman could. You might not believe me, but I have videos catching Caleb in action. My girls have an Xbox and if there is a way to find music on any device, you'd better know ... Caleb will find it! One day he picked up the Xbox controller. On his own, he searched for the YouTube.com application. Finding it, he began to type in the name of an artist he listens to, Bryson Tiller. I know you're thinking, "No way!" But trust me, this picture-taking, video-recording mommy has proof! On another day, Caleb was at his barber getting his hair cut. He sometimes has to have a device in his hands — or a Dum Dum sucker — to sit through a haircut. This day, he was squirming around in the chair while using his tablet. Mike, his barber, was patient as usual, waiting for Caleb to settle down and at the same time, watching him type in the search window on YouTube.

"Precious," Mike said in astonishment, "Caleb is typing the word 'exchange,' which happens to be a song of Bryson Tiller's."

"I know. He's a pretty smart kid," I responded with a smile, my chest poked out a little.

Mike then left me with words I'm sure we all have heard before, but which meant something extra-special to me that day: "You never know who you are raising and what they may be." Those were the words I needed to hear.

I have been, and will always be, Caleb's Number One supporter. But I could no longer limit my son by feeling that other moms with able-bodied sons were better off than me, or that their sons' futures looked brighter than my son's future. I know it was not right to be envious of these other moms; they did nothing wrong.

I will always cheer Caleb on. I'll push him, guide him and encourage him every step of the way. I will always pray for him more than I pray for myself. I will always have some degree of uneasiness about the unknown, however, and therefore I will fight for Caleb until he shows me or tells me to do otherwise. You all should know and get ready, because one day my baby will be able to tell me, "Mommy, I found my voice. You can give yours a rest."

Dear God,

Today I bring to You my children. Please show me how to parent these precious gifts You have given me. Help me to be the best mother I can be. I pray that Your Holy Spirit will teach me, Your wisdom will guide me, and Your love will move me. Most of all, Lord, I give these children back to You. Amen.

The Words "Normal" and "Special"

Our society is rife with labels that are sometimes put on us. I truly do not like labels, especially if they make someone feel superior or inferior to the next person. Just a few examples of labels: stupid, gay, retarded, skinny, fat. Horrible words!

Words can have an adverse effect on people and their lives in ways we could not even imagine. Take suicide, for instance. It's the third leading cause of death among young people, resulting in about 4,400 deaths per year, according to the Centers for Disease Control. For every suicide, there are at least 100 suicide attempts. More than 14 percent of high school students have considered suicide, and almost 7 percent have attempted it. Reasons for these suicides include bullying — the use of words for the intimidation and humiliation of others, whether verbal or written (cyberbullying).

Putting labels on others may be subtler, but the effects can be just dehumanizing. I think about two words in particular: NORMAL and SPECIAL. These are words I have heard throughout all my 33 years, but after my son Caleb was born they seemed to be constantly in use, either by me or by someone else. I honestly could do without these two words.

I know you're thinking: *Precious, you are crazy. They are just words. What's the big deal?*

A Piece of My Puzzle

Here's the big deal. The word "special" came up in conversations, used as if my Caleb were an alien from outer space whose special powers were difficulties in behavior, social interaction, communication and sensory sensitivities. The word "normal" was used to describe everyone on Planet Earth who did not have a visible or documented disability. This annoyed me to no end. Even people close to me overuse the word "special." These are the same people who feel the need to insert the phrase "special-needs kid" in every conversation instead of simply referring to the child as a little boy or little girl. Some of these people rudely state their opinion that the child will never be able to take part in life in a "normal" way.

I am in no way here to judge anyone. I simply speak from a mother's point of view ... a mother of a little boy who happens to have autism. We mothers of autistic children are not in denial. We know our children have special needs; we do not need anyone to remind us of this. Trust me when I say we have asked ourselves "What?" "How?" and "Why?" over and over when it came to our babies.

Furthermore, we do not need anyone to compare our babies to any child ... period. There are no two children alike! I'll give the perfect example. My sister Tanisha gave birth to twin girls. As of this writing, these girls were 6 years old. Granted, they were fraternal twins, but my nieces Chasity and Chrissette are complete opposites despite sharing the same womb for about 37 weeks. Chasity, the eldest, is the twin we always say has been here before. She has an "old soul" and loves talking. She's the shorter one. Chrissette, who's taller, is more laid back. I also know of *identical* twins who have different personalities, diverse ways of thinking, different ways of doing things.

My point is this: We must watch our choice of words when it comes to children who have disabilities. They *are* paying attention, as are other children ... especially when children with disabilities are labeled in a negative way. These babies deserve to be regarded first and foremost as *children*. Take a moment and look at these amazing children before you note their disabilities. As an autism advocate, I work hard to encourage this to the fullest.

As an autism advocate, I also work hard to put myself and my family out there in hopes that other families can feel secure in the knowledge that they are not going through this life-changing situation alone. There are so many wonderful resources that are affordable, if not free, to parents of children with disabilities.

I promise to continue to my part to educate my family and others about autism. It has changed our lives immensely, but I thank God for all the help along the way.

O God, we have so many ways of drawing lines between us — GENDER & SEXUAL PREFERENCE, race & nationalities, political parties & philosophies, social status & economic classes, gifted & challenged. .... Help us, O God, to see one another through your eyes. To remember that there is room for EVERYONE at the foot of the cross. ... May we become mirrors of Your LOVE — a LOVE that transcends lines and labels and differences — to each and every person we encounter today. Amen.

— Phil Ferrara, Sr.

It's OK to *Not* be OK All the Time

Fall down seven times, stand up eight. This is one of my favorite Japanese proverbs.

We hear so many times, "You have to be strong for your kids. You have to set an example of a strong woman/parent. There is no room to be weak and feel sorry for yourself. You are not allowed to throw yourselves pity parties." Here is my response — are you ready? WE ARE NOT ROBOTS. WE ARE HUMAN BEINGS. WE WILL MAKE MISTAKES.

Now that I have your attention, I'll ditch the capital letters. If we were to never express our emotions in one way or another, that would be a recipe for disaster. It is very unhealthy to mask those feelings, bury them or even substitute them for something else. Trust me. I am a living example of someone who has held things in that have bothered her, only to release them at the wrong time and on the wrong people. So I say, loudly and proudly, that it is *more* than OK to not be OK all the time!

After two years at Caleb's school, I decided to leave my job there because I was starting to feel overwhelmed. I was with my students all day long, Monday through Friday, not to mention the fact that I was working *two* jobs … as a teacher *and* a home health aide. I still had to go home each day to my baby boy and make sure he stayed on his schedule at home. Balancing life with my daughters and Caleb, and working with children with special needs all day every day, had begun to take a toll.

Because I was no longer an employee at Caleb's school, the extended-care cost there was out of my budget, and the drive there was a long one. So, I chose to search for another school. Now Caleb had been at Pediatrics Plus before he was diagnosed; the quality of the teachers, nurses, and therapists was beyond what any parent could ask for. Although there was an uneasiness in the bottom of my stomach, Caleb and I toured several other schools. Suffice it to say, they were *not* Pediatrics Plus!

One Thursday, we had just returned home from touring one of these schools ... and my stress was working overtime. Physically, I was making Caleb's lunch, but mentally I was all over the place. Caleb requested a honey bun, one of his favorite snacks. Now Caleb eats his honey buns one way only: He turns them sideways and bites them in the middle. He does not like for his honey bun to be broken into pieces. But before I knew it, I had absent-mindedly broken Caleb's honey bun in half. I just *knew* he was going to go into full distress, and I was not prepared mentally for this.

Caleb took the pieces of his honey bun and attempted several times, with all his little might, to put them back together.

"Caleb, Baby, it's OK. You can't put that honey bun back together, son," I told him.

But he went on trying to "repair" his honey bun. He even tried forcing the two halves together while biting at the same time, but they fell apart. He looked at the two pieces on the table, where they had landed. Finally, he picked one up, finished eating it, then reached for the other one and ate it also.

I am a firm believer that God sometimes shows us things in funny ways ... and sometimes, He uses our children to get our attention.

A Piece of My Puzzle

On that day, He chose to use my son and his honey bun to teach me four great lessons: (1) not everything *can* be put back together; (2) everything *need* not be put back together the way we think it should be; (3) not everything needs to be put back together at all; and (4) in time, everything will be OK. When Caleb hit on this "new" way of eating his honey bun, I cried and laughed like a crazy person. I am sure he was thinking, *my mommy has totally lost her mind.*

That was not the first time I'd had an encounter, or shall I say a lesson, from God using food. April is Autism Awareness month; April 2 is National Autism Day. In 2017, I decided I was going to create a yearly tradition called "AuSome Kid Day." The autism awareness color is blue, so at the last minute, I was running around trying to find everything blue.

I found the perfect cake at the grocery store. A woman in the store's bakery personalized the cake for me. As she did, we talked. Her nephew was autistic also. She agreed with me that we should not have to always go online to purchase items for autistic children ... and that there should be aids on hand at public places — like grocery stores — for children with special needs. For instance, I would love to see carts that allow these children access to headphones that accommodate hearing sensitivity. I would also love to see a mandatory training for store employees that gives basic knowledge about various disabilities. This way, employees will know what is going on when they see a child kicking off his shoes, hitting himself in the head or screaming loudly; or sees a parent administering joint compressions (a compression, push or weight-bearing item applied to the shoulders, elbows, etc.) to help calm down the child. These are simple things that help spread knowledge, awareness, and acceptance into our world. And I would of course love to see at least one aisle, or section, in every store available containing items for children or individuals with special needs.

Back to Caleb's cake. I wanted two puzzle pieces to go on it, as puzzle pieces are a universal symbol of autism awareness. But the cake was perfect with just the words "Caleb Lamar, You're an AuSome Kid." I got the gut feeling that I should take a picture; unfortunately, I ignored it.

The cake was going to be served at a party at home; afterward, we were going to head out to this cool trampoline park. But not even an hour after I got home, Caleb decided he wanted to have a little piece of the cake, which was still in its box. As he tried to sample it, the box fell from the table to the floor, flipping the cake upside down in the process and ruining its design!

My feelings were hurt, to say the least. I have never been good at arts and crafts, and my penmanship is bad. But I tend to try to make everything perfect, so I attempted to rewrite the ruined message topping the cake. I am sure I made it worse. Then we heard thunder. There we were, with a flipped-over cake and a storm heading our way because April brings ... showers. So much for the trampoline park.

But once I was over the cake mishap, we had an enjoyable time anyway. I shared some of our pictures on Facebook. Two women friends commented that Caleb's cake was more fitting in its fallen/repaired state. "May God give you strength, courage, and the knowledge to help others, along with yourself," one commented. "He had to put Caleb's touch to it ... now it is perfect!" wrote the other. After reading their comments, I cried like a baby because I knew God was using Caleb, and them, to let me know once again that it's OK for everything not to always be OK. "Precious, enjoy the moments you are in," He was telling me.

That day was also special because friends and family helped us "light it up blue" in a major way by wearing blue and using the hashtags #AutismAwareness #AutismAcceptance #AutismAwarenessMonth #AutismAwarenessDay #DifferentNotLess and #TeamCalebLamar; they also used these hashtags for other AuSome (Autistic Kids) they knew. The love and support shown was beyond amazing!

I am still learning that everything does not have to be perfect, or go as planned, all the time. I should know that better than anyone in our #AuSomeWorldofAutism.

Do not worry ...

> *Therefore I tell you, do not worry about your life, what you will eat or drink; or about your body, what you will wear. Is not life more than food and the body more than clothes? Look at the birds of the air; they do not sow or reap or store away in barns, and yet your heavenly Father feeds them. Are you not much more valuable than they? Can any one of you by worrying add a single hour to your life? And why do you worry about clothes? See how the flowers of the field grow. They do not labor or spin. Yet I tell you that not even Solomon in his entire splendor was dressed like one of these. If that is how God clothes the grass of the field, which is here today and tomorrow is thrown into the fire, will he not much more clothe you — you of little faith? So do not worry, saying, 'What shall*

we eat?' or 'What shall we drink?' or 'What shall we wear?' For the pagans run after all these things, and your heavenly Father knows that you need them. But seek first his kingdom and his righteousness, and all these things will be given to you as well. Therefore do not worry about tomorrow, for tomorrow will worry about itself. Each day has enough trouble of its own.

— Matthew 6:34 (NIV)

Living Life as an Example

Have you ever run into someone you'd dated years earlier ... someone who tells you they were fools for letting you go and that you were a great catch? For many, that would be considered an ego stroke. Well, after this happened to me a few too many times, I began to wonder what I was attracting, what exactly was I entertaining, and most important, what these guys were seeing when they looked at me.

I would have my many cry sessions with my mother, asking her why God was so hard on me when it came to these relationships. She has never changed her response: "Those men were only in your life to procreate my beautiful grandbabies that you carried, birthed and are taking great care of. But you are not alone. You have God's help."

This made me furious! I was doing what I like to call "listening to respond," so I would say, "That makes no sense at all! You're basically telling me that I am only good enough to create life, not have a companion to love me and help me with these children?" It took more than several occasions and debates before I could understand — before I even wanted to understand — what my mother meant by her statement.

Think about the words *living life as an example*. I knew I was more than worth having someone to truly love me and be a part of my life as well as my children's lives. Things happen to us that are out of our control, but there are also consequences for our actions — and if I'm going to be honest, I'll have to admit that the consequences to my actions include being a single parent of three. This in no way absolves my children's fathers from any wrongdoing; it simply means that I, Precious, made some poor decisions, and I am living with the consequences. This is not me beating myself up; I am not the first single parent and I will not be the last. But I know that had I made better choices, my life would be different.

As things stand now, I am proud of who I have grown to be. My mistakes are just mistakes — nothing more, nothing less. I love my three children and I couldn't imagine my life without them.

I have had so many "want-to-dos." Other than advocating for autism, my heart's desire is to open a youth center for girls. I believe that if I could be transparent with these girls, sharing my experiences, my choices and my mistakes, they could somehow relate and take a better route in life than I took. I believe all girls deserve that happy ending. To me, living life as an example simply means I have gone through a lot of challenges and overcome a lot of them. I am still going through life's test and trials, but now I can use my personal knowledge and experiences to help other people. That alone makes me happy, so yes, I can honestly say I am OK with being a living, breathing, real-life example.

I am very thankful for my life and my story, because now I see it has never just been about me. The bigger picture has always been about helping others while helping myself ... what I like to call a "lesson in a lesson."

As I stated in the previous chapter, April is Autism Awareness Month and April 2 is Autism Awareness Day. But I do what I can to spread awareness and acceptance for autism throughout the year. When I reactivated my social-network page, I decided I would use it only as a platform for this. Doing so would prevent me from using the page just to complain or vent about things in inappropriate ways. I am sure many people prefer to see drama, but I would rather be more positive.

The first picture I posted of Caleb and me, I was wearing a shirt bearing the statement, "I am his voice; he is my heart," and he was wearing a matching shirt with the statement, "She is my voice; I am her heart." These were shirts that a coworker had designed for us. The feedback and love were so amazing! Plus, I had the humbling experience of being recognized by Autism Speaks, an advocacy organization in the United States that sponsors autism research and conducts awareness and outreach activities aimed at families, governments, and the public. This organization posted Caleb's and my picture on its page — and yes, we were trending at 4.3K "likes!" The picture was perfect. It captured Caleb being unapologetically himself ... having a self-stimulatory behavior moment (also known as "stimming"). This allowed my coworker to profit also, because people were coming from everywhere wanting to order the shirts Caleb and I wore.

All that was super-cool and awesome, but here's what *really* touched me: I had a dad to message me. We were not friends on Facebook and did not know each other personally. But, because he'd seen our picture on the Autism Speaks page, he reached out with a message that touched my heart. He thanked me for spreading awareness and supporting the movement. He went on to say that it was a great feeling to see other families on this autism journey being so open. He told me he had a daughter who had been diagnosed with autism when she was 3. Seeing my post brightened his day, because they were having a rough morning. (Jonathan and I are now good friends; his daughter, Ava, is progressing and beating the odds of autism every day.)

I am far from being a leader or running any show when it comes to this autism journey. I, too, still have many days where I'm feeling alone and unsure of how to handle things. I now understand that Caleb and I are like many other families. We are a living example and an answer to questions. We represent a fresh of breath air, or reason to exhale, to families of children who have just been diagnosed, families who do not have a clue as to where to start. I am OK with being in the forefront, even though it makes me very nervous at times to know that people are watching us. But it makes me happy to know that my family can help, and possibly is helping, someone in need. I am OK with being a living example.

Let your light so shine before men, that they may see your good works, and glorify your Father which is in heaven.

— Matthew 5:16 (KJV)

Balancing Life with Your Other Kids

You do not have to be the parent of a child with special needs to understand that you must properly balance life with your kids. I try to make sure I am sharing quality time equally with each of my three. Granted, I am still learning how to perfect that balance, especially as my daughters get older. They like and dislike different things every day, it seems. I guess that's how it goes when you have a 15-year-old, an 11-year-old and a 4-year-old in your home. A technique I have learned, and with which I have not gone wrong, is letting them enjoy a favorite activity each week/weekend.

(I know you are wondering how that works when Caleb is diagnosed as nonverbal. Thing is, Caleb is more than capable of communicating *nonverbally*. We all know we will be listening to music, jumping on our trampoline or playing in shaving cream at some point, and trust me, we would never exclude him. He wouldn't let us! Caleb makes his presence known.)

Now I have not always been on what I call my B+ game. I try to have conversation time with my girls quite often, asking the questions they like to skim through, such as "How was school?" or "What did you learn different today?" During one of our many sessions, my eldest asked whether I was asking some of these questions out of routine, or if I really wanted to know. There went my gut punch! She did not pose her question in a disrespectful manner. But I realized that if she was asking, she must have felt that I didn't really have anything meaningful to discuss with her.

I really did not know how to answer the question — my best answer would have been "both," and that may not have made any sense to her.

So now, my conversations with both girls start with my asking what *they* would like to talk about. I still ask those same questions I used to ask, just not in the same order or manner.

Balancing life with kids can be a considerable challenge for a working single mom. Here is how I try to balance life in my household: I work from 8:30 a.m. to 3 p.m. each weekday, which means I leave the house before my girls do. I drop Caleb off at school, then head to work. We do not have time to have breakfast together. The kids grab items on the way out the door or eat breakfast at school; I pick something up on my way to work. I do, however, tell them, "I love you guys; have a good day. Do not forget to pray." Then we are off to start our day. If no errands or other matters command our attention when we make it home, our evening consists of dinner, homework, baths and bed. The next day, it starts all over again.

I know it all seems rushed and crazy. If I could create a twin me, I would make sure my children awakened every morning to the smell of breakfast ... and I would personally see each child off to school. Unfortunately, I have missed many awards ceremonies and field trips because I had to work. Our weekends are much more laid back; we can take time to look into each other's eyes and love each other.

This is not a perfect situation. But it is our reality until this mommy wins the lottery.

Balancing life will be a different experience for each family, depending on that family's financial situation and whether there is one parent or two in the home. I know all too well the guilt that comes with working long hours, and working two jobs, to provide for a family. What helps me is the knowledge that I must work to ensure that my family's needs are met.

But the most important thing we, as parents, want to do is make adequate time for our children so that they don't feel neglected. It's important to me that my kids have new experiences, so in March of 2017, we took a road trip for the first time ... a seven-hour drive with only a couple of stops. (That was huge deal, considering I had a then-2-year-old!) We decided we needed some beach time so for spring break, so we traveled to Gulf Shores, Ala. We celebrated Caleb's third birthday and spring break, all in one trip. It was worth it just to see the joy on my children's faces ... in fact, it was priceless! Countless times, my daughters told me they were just glad to be out of the house and out of town. Needless to say, I earned some major "mommy points"! Now, traveling is our thing.

Again, balancing life with your kids isn't easy, especially if you're single, have a child with special needs and don't have the luxury of being a stay-at-home mom. But it's by no means impossible.

Dating as a Single Mom with a Special-Needs Child

Dating is on my list of scary things, right up there with clowns, spiders and snakes. The idea was foreign to me for a long time.

Let me try to be clearer. To me, dating someone involves meeting that person for dinner and a movie and talking, by phone and in person … sharing family stories, likes, dislikes, goals and common interests. When you both agree that things are getting serious, you make plans to meet each other's families. But in the 21st century, this is not how dating goes down. It goes down via DM (Direct Message) on social-media sites, where people skip the "getting to know you" phase — sending each other nude or suggestive photos and "hooking up" sexually. I am certainly not perfect. I have failed at this dating thing, which is exactly why I say it's foreign to me.

Dating becomes even more intense when one or both partners comes as a "package deal," which means there are kids involved. I have three children, two of them girls. Girls always pay close attention to how their mothers talk or behave. We are on the front lines as our daughters' first role models. Then I have a 3-year-old son who has autism and requires much of my time. So, when a man comes into our world, it's a guarantee that we will uproot everything he has and flip it over!

"I have to tell you that we are a fun bunch of people, but it's not always easy," I've told would-be suitors. "Just make sure you want to deal with my super-awesome family before approaching this mommy." Luckily my current boyfriend, James, blends in with us very well.

At one time, dating was also difficult in that I was carrying extra baggage from previous experiences and relationships. My childhood best friend, Likera, and I would sit on the phone for hours at a time, trying to figure out how our ex-Mr. Wrongs could have ever felt comfortable approaching us in the first place. That inevitably led to our asking, "What are we attracting? What are we advertising?"

This is a subject I brought up earlier, in passing. Let me explain further: You are your own advertising agency. When people first meet you, what "vibes" do they get from you? When people see you, do they see someone who looks happy, or do you always look angry or unapproachable? How do you smell? (I ask this because perfume and cologne are often conversation starters for potential partners — "Where did you purchase that fragrance?") Do you dress appropriately for the occasion? If you are going to a business venue, you would not wear a miniskirt and crop top, would you? This is what I mean when I say that we are all advertising something. I have now concluded that I was sending mixed advertisements, because I dated a lot of "mixture guys." A mixture guy is a guy who initially seems to be a good catch: good-looking. Book smart. Street smart. Able to hold down some type of employment. But he's also mentally unstable. Has substance-abuse issues. Has no clue as to what a healthy, long-term relationship looks like because he previously engaged only in temporary hookups.

Before I met James, I was dating for all the wrong reasons. I had still not learned my lesson. I was not dating for companionship;

I was trying to get over someone else. *Do not show your real feelings,* I'd tell myself. *Do not be available all the time; that's too needy. Get what you need from them and keep it moving, girl.* This was my childish way of protecting myself from getting hurt again. I was so focused on making sure I was following all my rules, I was not even getting to know my suitors properly, and that was not fair to them or myself. I found myself even comparing guys. Who was I to be doing all this, as if I was perfect and had my life together?

I kept my baggage near me at all times ... my mental and emotional baggage, that is. I carried around trust issues, which meant that anything that was said to me I took with a grain of salt. I carried around negative thoughts, judgment, games and lies ... until, one day, I started to feel something for James. Our conversations were never forced; they seemed to flow naturally. We shared things with each other — you know, those things you share when you are trying to really get to know one another. I appreciated his consistency and the fact that he was knowledgeable about autism.

Not every day has been easy or perfect. When you have been through some life-changing challenges, you tend to have a harder time opening up and accepting new things. But I thank God for bringing James into my life at the right time for the right reasons. I am looking forward to continuing our present and building our future together.

Being your authentic self helps you become a better entrepreneur, leader, and human. It's not easy, though: From an early age people, especially young men, are often encouraged to hide their emotions, put on a brave face, and not cry. In effect, we're taught *not* to be authentic. I have played cover-up for many years, but now it's time to unmask myself, be transparent and live as my true, happy self. I am OK with being someone who has made many, *many* mistakes. I have experienced love, grief, hurt, anger … every emotion you can name, I'm sure I've felt!

I want people to know that they need not be ashamed of the things we go through. They build our character. I hope my story can one day help someone who needs help.

Am I now trying to win the approval of human beings, or of God? Or am I trying to please people? If I were still trying to please people, I would not be a servant of Christ.

— Galatians 1:10 (NIV)

Do nothing out of selfish ambition or vain conceit. Rather, in humility value others above yourselves

— Philippians 2:3 (NIV)

Get Off the Guilt Train

ALL ABOARD!!! We all have felt guilty about one thing or another, whether it's that extra piece of cheesecake we ate when we knew we did not need it, or that New Year's resolution we did not keep (I *know* we are all guilty of that one!). Were I in a 12-step program for Guilt Anonymous, I would introduce myself like this: "Hello, my name is Precious Tameka Weatherspoon and I am guilty of holding onto people and situations longer than I'm supposed to."

Have you ever heard the saying that people and situations are sometimes meant to last only for a season, and when their season is up, they will leave? I have the hardest time with that one, simply because I have a tough time opening up to people. When I do open up and the relationship fails, I tend to wonder whether I was the reason ... not a good feeling at all. This leads me to my next guilt trip: guilt for expressing disapproval to those who have done me wrong. How does the saying go — "It's a curse and a blessing to have a good heart"? There is some truth to that.

I know I have hurt people in situations I will probably never get to fix. I *know* I won't get to fix things with my Aunt Vera, who passed away from cancer in 2017. Aunt Vera was my dad's baby sister; everyone in our small hometown of Blytheville, AR, knew and loved her. But Aunt Vera could hold onto grudges ... and she was angry at me. I couldn't even remember why. She told my sister it was because I'd once promised I would give her a ride somewhere but had failed to keep my word. Days turned into

A Piece of My Puzzle

weeks, weeks turned into months, months turned into years … and my aunt remained angry. Once, after her cancer diagnosis, she came to my sister's home while I was there and "short-worded" me, speaking only when necessary and making no attempt at any other conversation.

As Aunt Vera became more ill, I promised myself I would travel to Blytheville to visit her. But time was not on my side. When I saw her again, she was in the hospital and on a ventilator. With tears streaming down my face, I finally told my aunt that I was sorry and that she had better not still be mad at me. It still seems unreal that she is gone, and I will not ever get to hear her voice again or tell her how sorry I am. I'm reminded ever so often of how I missed many opportunities to just hug her and apologize. I am still praying for peace about that situation.

I have been riding the guilt train for a long time now and am learning that I am only one person. I now understand that there are some situations from which I cannot always get closure. I have started journaling about those situations that haunt me the most, acknowledging my errors and working hard to not repeat them. I will accept the fact that doing my part is simply all I can do; I am not responsible for other people's actions or attitudes. And I will forgive myself.

I read an article that showed me that I was a perfect definition for "guilt allergy" — meaning I can't stomach the feeling of guilt. I am a prime target for a guilt tripper. In fact, the guilt tripper, like a dog, can sniff out weakness. But luckily for me and others like me, there is a solution. We have to build up what is called our emotional muscle. In other words, we must get tougher and stop taking on battles that can simply be dismissed. I am guilty for giving too much of my attention to things, situations and people.

It's like staying to see a surgeon in action. You keep hiding your eyes because of the cutting and bleeding, but you don't want to leave because you just *have* to know what the end will look like.

Remember, no behavior continues without it being fed. When the feeding stops, the behavior stops.

Not all guilt trips have to do with relationships. You could be suffering from guilt for being a parent of a sweet baby boy who happens to be autistic. I have ridden this train since May 31, 2015 — the date Caleb was diagnosed. I asked myself such questions as, *Did I stress to much? Did I eat something wrong? Did I not eat enough of something?* The questions are endless, and many are unanswered. I now look at my Caleb Lamar, and I ask myself, *does being on this guilt trip change his diagnosis? Am I helping anything by staying on this guilt trip?* The answer is no, not at all! My time has expired. I have reached my destination. Time to get off the guilt train and start focusing on important things ... and people, my children being first and foremost. (It took me a long time to understand that saying, "In order to truly know love, you have to experience pain." The best examples of it, for me, were the three times I gave birth. Each time, it was too late to receive any pain medications. I naturally pushed out each child ... a 6-pound girl, then a 7-pound girl, then an 8-pound baby boy, so I know about pain. But it's pain for which I will forever be grateful, because I was given three blessings in return.)

In life we will all make mistakes. But we should never allow our mistakes to define us, even though some of those mistakes are costlier than others. We can use our mistakes to become wiser. God will always remain faithful to His children. I thank Him for favor and grace.

A Piece of My Puzzle

Are *you* learning from your mistakes? Do you continue to dwell on them? Forget your past mistakes and keep moving toward the eternal prize. God is always with you. He will restore and strengthen you. I know it is often easier said than done. But in school, the teacher or professor sometimes allows us to redo a test if we fail it. God will do the same with our life mistakes until we learn the lesson and make a change. We are always so worried about our past mistakes, we forget that we can start to make a change in the present! Whether it was a sin or an unwise decision, God will bring you through it, just as He has done for me.

I have made many mistakes, some of which cost me a lot, but now I do not regret them. Although they caused me to suffer, sometimes to the point of discouragement, I became more dependent on the Lord. The strength I thought I no longer had, I rediscovered. And I still have that strength ... in fact, it has magnified. I can continue to push through life's many tests and trials because I have found peace in Christ. God used the bad things in my life for good; I matured spiritually, becoming more obedient, praying more and gaining wisdom. Now I can help others make better life choices.

Character cannot be developed in ease and quiet. Only through experience of trial and suffering can the soul is strengthened, ambition inspired, and success achieve.

— Helen Kelle

Taking It One Day at a Time

God, give us grace to accept with serenity
the things that cannot be changed,

Courage to change the things

which should be changed,

and the Wisdom to distinguish

the one from the other.

Living one day at a time,

Enjoying one moment at a time,

Accepting hardship as a pathway to peace,

Taking, as Jesus did,

This sinful world as it is,

Not as I would have it,

Trusting that You will make all things right,

If I surrender to Your will,

So that I may be reasonably happy in this life,

A Piece of My Puzzle

And supremely happy with You forever in the next.

Amen.

— Reinhold Niebuhr

(Complete, Unabridged, Original Version)

It was time to take back my life ... a cliché, I know, but that's the best description for what I did.

I began by making this note to myself every morning before getting out of bed: I REFUSE TO GIVE SO MUCH OF MY ENERGY TO THE THINGS IN MY LIFE THAT ARE NOT GOING WELL.

"I need my peace back now!" I said to myself. "I am through being the victim."

The victimhood I'd decided to shed began with my feelings about Caleb's dad. I was at fault for allowing him to treat this special gift from God like an option, when Caleb was a priority. I was fed up with worrying about what people would say and think.

I took back something valuable that Caleb's father had held onto for a long time and treated like trash ... MY HEART. I made the decision to detach myself from him emotionally and get off the rollercoaster on which he'd had Caleb and me riding for more than three years. He just would not know what he'd missed out on in Caleb's life.

I must be honest; the detachment did not go smoothly, and it hurt like hell. But I needed to say, "Yes, this is my life." I needed to ask God to forgive me for thinking that He had left my side and did not care. God was simply letting me throw my fit, waiting patiently for me to come to Him, give Him my problems fully, and leave them there with Him. I realized that I was the only one who could get me through my tests and trials … but not without with God's help, and I was ready for that help. So many people and opportunities had presented themselves for Caleb and my family to benefit from. I would have been a fool to continue to hold onto this toxic attachment that was taking precious time and moments from my son and me.

My new prayer was this: *God, heal me from the inside out, and guard my thoughts from anything that is not healthy. Help me to know that my emotional illness is not a permanent situation and that I can be free from this completely. God, when You heal me, make me better, not bitter. I choose to live a happy, healthy life for myself and my kids, and I will accept Your will, no matter what it may be. In Jesus' name I pray, Amen.*

I knew it was going to take some time for me to fully forgive Caleb's dad and not revisit the hurt, but I prayed that God would have mercy on his soul. I had cried so much, and I didn't want to waste any more tears. I would instead save my tears for happy moments, like when my Caleb overcame another challenge or obstacle. I would save these tears for when my Caleb was able and ready to express himself with words. With God I had everything I needed.

I also decided to take my life back by putting away worry. Instead, I pray each day for Caleb to be covered in every area of his life so that he will have a healthy, successful future. It is so easy to fall into the worry trap, especially in times of trial. A typical human response to bad news is to move automatically into a state of worry and anxiety. We get ahead of ourselves, and ahead of God, as we attempt to predict the many ways a trial may pan out.

But Philippians 4:6 clearly tells us: *Do not be anxious about anything, but in every situation, by prayer and petition, with thanksgiving, present your requests to God* (NIV).

Being Open to New Ways of Thinking and Reacting

Throughout our lives, we are influenced by many different people and things I, for instance, grew up in a Christian home with a mother who was a minister. Sundays were reserved for church, and Wednesday evenings for Bible study — my sister and I were not given a choice. Participating in church activities and programs was also a priority.

I'll be honest: Often, I was quite upset at being made to participate! I felt like I had no voice and was prevented from making any decisions for myself. Now older and wiser, I understand why my mother made us attend these services and programs. This was her way of keeping us on the right path. We were taught how to live a lifestyle that would help us make proper decisions when we became adults.

Every morning before school, my mother would pray with my sister and me. She also anointed our heads with oil that had been prayed over. At the time, my sister and I felt like our mother was keeping us from getting ready for school — or, shall I say, get in the mirror and primp. And it annoyed us when she left our foreheads with oil stains that we had to wipe away.

I did not start trying to fully understand why my mother raised us the way she did until I decided to seek a personal relationship with God. I realize that people hold varying religious beliefs, and that is fine. But throughout my 33 years on this earth, I have been in situations that I would never have overcome had it not been for God, along with the Christian foundation my mother laid for me.

We parents of children who have special needs usually feel that we need to correct every mistake and fix every problem, big or small, when it comes to our babies. I can attest to the fact that it is extremely hard to *think* before *reacting* when it comes to protecting our babies, defending them and making sure they are getting everything they need. Many of our babies are unable to share their feelings verbally. That leaves us, the parents or caregivers, to jump in. We are more than ready to do so ... and often we do it with such force, we come off as overanxious or overprotective.

I have begun trying to look through the eyes of others when they see those who have disabilities. Despite autism awareness efforts, there remain many who know nothing about the disorder and don't know the proper things to say or do when they are around autistic children and their families. Therefore, I decided to change my reaction to inappropriate comments or actions made in ignorance — it's exhausting to keep getting angry. I urge all parents in my shoes to make this decision. We can be advocates and spread awareness of our children's condition, but we must remember that there are many ways to do this. We will still come across those people who will have us thinking, *did you really just say that? Wow, are you really doing that?* And we will be tempted to wonder whether common sense is really all that common! We must remember that the best thing we can do is to continue to spread knowledge about the autism spectrum ... all aspects of it. We should be working to make sure that resources are more readily available.

Keeping an open mind and learning *how* to react to people's reactions to our children will go far in decreasing our feelings of frustration and helplessness. Have you ever been in a situation in which you were sure you knew the way to solve a problem … yet the problem kept cropping back up? In such a situation, you needed to be open to new ways of thinking and reacting. Albert Einstein is widely credited with saying, "The definition of insanity is doing the same thing over and over again and expecting different results." The interesting thing is that, according to autism expert Simon Baron-Cohen, Albert Einstein showed signs of Asperger syndrome, defined as a form of autism. I think we all should realize that if we want to see a change in the way people approach, treat and think about individuals who are on the autism spectrum, we must try different approaches to reaching *them*.

Here are two scriptures I will leave you with:

A soft answer turns away wrath, but a harsh word stirs up anger.

— Proverbs 15:1 (ESV)

As for the one who is weak in faith, welcome him, but not to quarrel over opinions. One person believes he may eat anything, while the weak person eats only vegetables. Let not the one who eats despise the one who abstains, and let not the one who abstains pass judgment on the one who eats, for God has welcomed him. Who are you to pass judgment on the servant of another? It is before his own master that he stands or falls. And he will be upheld, for the Lord is able to make him stand.

— Romans 14:1-4 (ESV)

Listening Without Words

Look into my eyes and hear what I'm not saying, for my eyes speak louder than my voice ever will

— *Unknown*

Hearing the specialists say that Caleb is considered nonverbal put my "mommy radar" on an all-time high. That meant I had to pay extra-close attention to everything concerning Caleb. I would do a body search of him every day after he came home from school, or whenever he went anyplace else without me. I knew he had great teachers and was being well taken care of, but it made me sad to know that he would be unable to speak for himself when, or if, something happened to him.

Caleb had been blessed with some of the best therapists. As they worked with him, he began to show great progress. (He now uses sign language; "please" and "more" are his favorite words to sign.) When I worked at Caleb's school, I enjoyed the benefit of being able to peek in his classroom and check on him. I would see Caleb working and paying attention appropriately. But when we made it home, it was a different story. If he was off schedule and off his routine, it was like a circus in my house! I had no clue how to incorporate his school schedule into his home schedule. Yes, I was an educator and yes, I was working with special-needs children every day. But Caleb was not my student; he was my son.

And I learned early on that these kids' disabilities do not take away from their unique personalities! My Caleb came with a high dose of stubbornness and a strong tendency to test his limits when Mommy said "no" ... especially during one of his many IEP meetings. (An IEP, or individualized education program, is a written statement for a child with a disability that is developed, reviewed and revised in keeping with certain requirements based on laws and regulations.)

I learned from my favorite occupational therapist and speech therapist that I needed to meet Caleb where he was. I was putting too much emphasis on where I wanted him to be, instead of focusing on what he was already trying to do, or capable of doing well ... another lesson from God, in my opinion, that I needed to hear.

My son benefited from the help of visual schedules, along with his sisters being the great "Caleb whisperers." My daughters could literally get Caleb to do anything, and I loved it! I began to release the reins a little. Instead of pulling away from me, Caleb began listening to Mommy more. Actually, he was teaching me how to help him by paying attention to his gestures and signs.

Specialists speak of a persistent stereotype concerning people with autism; they're seen as lacking empathy and unable to understand emotion. It's true that many people with autism do not show emotion in ways that others would recognize. But the notion that people with autism generally lack empathy and cannot recognize feelings is absolutely wrong! One day I was in my room, listening to a gospel song that touched me so much that I began to cry. Caleb just happened to be in my room. His reaction made for the sweetest, most unexpected moment ever. He got right in my face, touched my eyes with his little hands, and laid

A Piece of My Puzzle

his head on my shoulder. Of course, that made me cry even more, just for a different reason. In that sweet moment we shared, Caleb showed me that words are not always needed to convey understanding and care.

Every day I learned something new from Caleb, patience being at the top of the list. Autistic nonverbal kids use their hands to point to and gesture at what they want. Often, Caleb would get so frustrated with us because we were taking too long to figure out his requests! He would flap his hands up and down so vigorously, he looked like he was about to take flight! But as time went on, Caleb gained the ability to use eye contact for most of his request. His main requests are for cereal, his drinking cup and his favorite foods — macaroni and cheese and, of course, honey buns. That may seem small, but progress is progress.

Some might think that having a nonverbal child in our home makes for a calm, quiet atmosphere. Quite the opposite! We are a loud bunch, especially when we are excited about something. We are all music lovers. Caleb is the official DJ, wanting to play music even when we are not in the mood. We have to tell him, "Caleb, you need your headphones, buddy."

Life is too ironic to fully understand sometimes. It takes sadness to know what happiness is, noise to appreciate silence, and absence to value presence.

Autism Is a Journey! Wear Your Seat Belt

The ultimate measure of a man is not where he stands in the moments of comfort and convenience, but where he stands at times of challenge and controversy.

— *Martin Luther King Jr.*

This quote hangs on the wall in my study room, where I can see it during those times I really need motivating. I encourage families that are on this autism journey to find whatever motivational aids work for them, whether they be inspirational quotes, songs or even pictures. I believe in having whatever one needs to get through those tough times.

Autism is a journey. You can plan everything perfectly, even trivial things, yet you must realize that things may not always go as planned. Our babies are not robots, and they may not care about Mommy's or Daddy's plans. If they are upset or bored, get ready for them to make it known. (Think about it: Everyone voices their opinion in one way or another, so why can't they?) I have so many stories of how I have planned things for my family, only for Caleb to add to the plans or take away from them.

I do not mean to paint autism strictly with a negative brush. This is not the image I am trying to convey. I am simply trying to say that you, as a parent of an autistic child, need to know your limits and always have a back-up plan. Never feel guilty about things not going as you'd planned them to go.

A Piece of My Puzzle

If you have other children, always get them involved in activities with your autistic child as much as possible. I am blessed to have two daughters who are very understanding and easygoing when it comes to things of this nature. I make sure they have girls' days out, because I do not want them to feel like there's Caleb, then them ... I have three beautiful kids, period.

I know everyone's family dynamics are different, culturally and otherwise. I just want to make it clear that no matter what, we are a community — a link of different individuals with kids or loved ones on every end of the autism spectrum. Our main focus is to spread awareness and acceptance while making sure we are lifting each other up. We are an important link in the autism community. Every time we share a quote, a story or an experience, no matter how simple, we are giving someone hope.

I am amazed that after three years of being on this autism journey, I now have the special "mommy autism radar" I'd mentioned earlier. (You will too, dads, siblings, and grandparents.) I want to be clear: I am not walking around judging these children or trying to diagnose them, especially when I am not in a position to do so. I am simply saying that I now am sensitive enough to notice the child in the supermarket who's flapping his hands, or the child at the doctor's office who does not want shoes on with his socks. Yes, I am aware that once you have met *one* individual on the autism spectrum, that is just that — no two people are the same. (I tell my Caleb all the time that he has some really cool, super-AuSome powers, and that I wish that Mommy had some also.)

I look forward to building relationships with families whose loved ones are on all ends of the autism spectrum. One thing I want to share — and of which I must remind myself of daily —

is this: As parents and caregivers over these babies, we can get too fixated on their disabilities and on such matters as IEPs and goals. *Wait, but this chapter says to make sure you are wearing your seat belt,* you may be thinking. I said that because it is true. There will be times when you are feeling overwhelmed, feel like you are falling apart. At times like those, you will need that seat belt.

Then there are times when we must take the seatbelt off or (loosen it just a little) and, first and foremost, allow our babies to just be themselves! If we do this, we will eliminate a lot of stress and many worries. Yes, we will have to have plans A, B, and C in place sometimes, but that is OK. Relax. Inhale and exhale as much as you need to. Know in your heart and mind that you are doing everything you can to ensure that your loved one is living a happy life, filled with wonderful experiences and memories.

Lastly, you should never feel guilty for needing a break or asking for help. Remember, as a parent of a child with autism, you are not alone ... you are part of an extended family whose members are all over the world. I personally think the autism community is an AuSome, AuMazing group of people!

Putting the Pieces Together

As the parent of a child with special needs, I cannot help but be an overemotional ball of overprotectiveness most (well, *all*) of the time. I have decided that this is not a flaw ... it's my job. I must be Caleb's voice until he finds his own. I must be Caleb's eyes until he can tell me what he sees. I must be wise and very discerning of the people I allow around my child, because he cannot tell me how they treat him. I must be Caleb's advocate on every front, because this is the sacred calling the Lord has hand-picked for me.

Looking back over Caleb's three years of life, I have to say I would have never thought we would be where we are now. Again, my daughters and I have learned so much from him — this little guy teaches us patience, unconditional love and how to keep our sense of humor. And I love that my daughters are doing their own research of autism. They get excited about sharing with me the things they have learned. I saw a meme somewhere that read: "If you want to know how to treat a child with autism... look to their siblings; they will show you." The tears came when I saw this meme because it was so fitting. As the "Caleb whisperers," Darryana and Jayla are so good with him, and so patient! I love the bond they share. (My oldest wisecracks that she can't wait until Caleb is older so that she can make him fetch things for her.)

Because I'm such a vocal advocate for autism awareness, other families on the autism journey occasionally reach out to me with questions and words of gratitude. These families tell me how relieved they are to know that they are not in this alone. I, in turn, appreciate the support I have from friends and family. I love the fact that everyone to whom I'm connected wants to gain knowledge, and help spread awareness, of autism.

When I was a little girl, I thought I had my life all planned out. In short, I was going to get married, have two kids — a girl and a boy — and be a professional photographer. Well, I am so glad that God chose a different route for me. Despite all the roadblocks I faced and mistakes I made, I am grateful. Caleb leaves a good impression everywhere we go; his loving, gentle spirit puts a smile on so many faces.

Autism is not a curse; it is our blessing. My sister Tanisha said it best: My Caleb Lamar Harris was born a superhero. His super powers? Seeing the good in a person. Blocking out negative things and people without hesitation. And let's not even talk about his ability to truly live life without worrying about what anyone thinks about him! He is one AuSome little guy.

I am learning to enjoy putting the pieces to our family's puzzle together each day. If, for some reason, a piece doesn't fit that moment or that day, we will just try again until we figure it.

Being confident of this, that he who began a good work in you will carry it on to completion until the day of Christ Jesus.

— Phil. 1:6 (NIV)

Finding Peace and Living Life

Everyone has said this one time or another: "I just want to be happy and be at peace." There will always be happy moments, like the birth of a baby, an engagement, a wedding, a birthday. We are happy when we watch our babies overcoming challenges and reaching milestones. But as the saying goes, we cannot have rainbows without rain. We have also experienced those moments that were not so happy ... death, illness or a child diagnosed with a disability. I am learning that the things on which we focus dictate our moods. Sometimes, staying positive is easier said than done. We are not perfect ... as I've stated before, we are not robots. We are human beings with feelings and emotions.

However, we must learn to express ourselves in a way that is not emotion-based. We can't fly off the handle every time we are feeling attacked, or our loved ones are being pre-judged in some way, or when various situations arise that are not ideal. This is a "self-accomplishment" — meaning that no one can help us with this or do it for us. (People can encourage you until they are out of breath. But if you do not change how you deal with and work through challenges and trials, nothing else will change.)

We were not given this life just to share cookie-and-ice-cream moments with people. We must share those broken, bruising moments also. That's where our growth occurs; that's also how we can help and heal others. That alone should give us peace.

I encourage and challenge each person reading this to find at least three ways to find inner peace. Do not worry if the first three things you come up with do not do the trick. Feel free to change them until you find what *does* work for you.

To me, having peace means living in the moment, not expecting things to be perfect, and not being anxious about the future. My three children are my peace; they calm my inner storms and battles. My boyfriend is indeed the yin to my yang. My mother is my prayer warrior, my mentor and my counselor. My sister is my strategy-making, goal-planning, laughing-through-it-all partner. My close friends are my social go-to people. Having all these people in my circle is wonderful; I would not trade them for anything. But I am also working on finding out what Precious needs on her own to have peace and happiness. I know this will take time — Rome was not built in a day, right? There will be bumps and roadblocks along the way. But I am ready to face each challenge with God's help and the loving support I have from family and friends.

I've learned that I can do many things but *wanting* to do them makes an enormous difference. I am the single parent of three beautiful kids, one being a little boy who has autism. Nothing about my life will ever be easy, or as society says, normal. But as I think back, I realize that nothing about my life has ever been easy or normal. I have had my share of tests and trials. Now that I can understand the reasons behind them, I am at peace with them. This is my life and my family, and I am grateful that God saw fit to make me the caregiver and overseer of such precious cargo.

I do not have everything all figured out, and I *definitely* do not know what tomorrow brings for my family and me. All I know is that I am a reflection of my babies and I want them to forever see their mommy as someone who never gives up when things get difficult. I want them to know that hard work and determination pay off, and that there is a such a thing as overcoming limits.

For a long time, I only had three major puzzle pieces ... then God sent me a special piece on March 21, 2014 — my Caleb Lamar — and he fits perfectly. Our puzzle is far from being complete, but we now have the most important pieces we need to continue to move forward.

To those who took the time to read this book, I pray God gives each of you your heart's desire. I pray now that you have a better understanding of autism. Remember that no matter what we come across in life, there will always be someone who has been through it or is going through it. That someone may prove to be your comfort. Or you may just be the one who needs to give a comforting word or two ... so if you have a story, please do not keep quiet about it. Find your peace, keep it, and share your story boldly and proudly!

God bless you all.

You cannot find peace by avoiding life.

— Virginia Woolf

BIBLIOGRAPHY

Bullying and Suicide. (2015, July 07). Retrieved April 17, 2018, from http://www.bullyingstatistics.org/content/bullying-and-suicide.html

Jerry Bridges Quote - 5 Faces of Christian Pain | ChristianQuotes.info. (2014, November 19). Retrieved April 18, 2018, from https://www.christianquotes.info/images/jerry-bridges-quote-5-faces-christian-pain/#axzz5CzKBfv8p